New Morning of the Pasture

New Morning of the Pasture
Poetic Reflections of a Korean American Pastor

Rev. Manwoo A. Kim
Senior Pastor
First Korean Presbyterian Church of Philadelphia

The Hermit Kingdom Press
Cheltenham ♦ Seoul ♦ Bangalore ♦ Cebu

New Morning of the Pasture:
Poetic Reflections of a Korean American Pastor

ISBN 0-97238-641-6

Copyright © 2003 The Hermit Kingdom Press

All rights reserved.
No part of this book may be reproduced, in any form or by any means, without permission in writing from the publisher.

Write to:

The Hermit Kingdom Press
Suite 291
48 Regent Street
Cambridge
CB2 1FD
United Kingdom

Translated by Onyoo Elizabeth Kim, Esq.

http://www.TheHermitKingdomPress.com

*I dedicate this book to my father-in-law, Rev. In Sun Jun
who was martyred during the Korean War (June 25, 1950)
and to my mother-in-law
and to my parents, Rev. and Mrs. Hee Do Kim,
who served as the model for my pastoral ministry my whole life.*

Contents

Preface	ix
Acknowledgements	xi
"April Is"	13
"Building The Church"	14
"We In Christ"	16
"On Children's Lord's Day"	17
"Mother's Day Poem"	19
"Thanks Be To God"	21
"The Memorial Day"	23
"In The First Garden's Hillside"	25
"Wilderness Of The Middle East"	27
"The Lord Will Provide"	29
"A Bird Without Wings"	31
"Do You Believe In Hell?"	33
"Have You Heard?"	35
"In The Summer Plants Grow"	37
"Heart That Yearns After Grace"	39
"Prayer Support"	40
"A Word Of Welcome"	41
"Student For Christ"	43
"Let Us Exalt God's Holy Name"	45
"Like Farmers Over-Anxious"	47
"Night When Star Is Shining"	49
"Autumnal Fragrance Permeates"	51
"Autumn Is A Going Away Season"	53
"With Autumn's Drizzle Descending"	55
"The Earth's Axis Slanting"	57

"Autumn Rain"	59
"The Heart That Jesus Likes"	60
"The Final One Word Spoken"	62
"God The Father's Salvation Plan"	64
"Early In The Morning"	66
"Let Us Wholeheartedly Proclaim"	68
"New Day"	69
"Though Having Nothing To Offer"	70
"A Thankful Heart"	71
"A New Morning Has Brightened"	73
"If Wind Does Not Blow"	74
"The Day Of The General Assembly"	75
"Because So Dirty and Filthy"	77
"As Christmas Fast Approaches"	79
"As King Of Kings"	81
"As On First Christmas' Dawn"	83
"Though Wanting To Go Back"	85
"The Harvest Of The New Heaven And The New Earth"	87
"Harvesting Church In This Land"	89
"A New Morning Of Daybreak"	91
"Last Night"	93
"The Winter Sea"	94
"Winter Night"	96
"Winter Tree"	98
"Though Large Flakes Of Snow Covered"	100
"Selecting Ordained Deacons"	102
"Today Is A Happy Day"	103
"Spring, Spring, Spring"	105
Rev. Manwoo A. Kim's Photos	107
"The Korean Diaspora's Realized Vision"	109

Preface

I give thanks, praise, honor, exaltation and glory to the living, loving and powerful God the Father!

Writing poetry is putting heart's feelings and emotions into words. Only with emotions coming from God's control of the heart, thought, and mind according to His perfect will can one sing spiritual songs. Whenever I read the Psalms in the Bible, I wanted to praise as such, and when I read the Old Testament prophecies, the beautiful words of revelation seemed to me as extremely exquisite songs. Whenever I read the Gospels or the historical books in the Holy Scriptures, God's wonderful acts seemed so poetic, and Jesus' life appeared to me as sacred heavenly music. The sentiment arising from reading about the vibrant and unfathomable lives of Moses, David and Paul among others moved my heart. The footprints of failures and successes, despair and restoration in their lives were a form of holy pilgrimage for me.

In my life also were many twists and turns. I always pondered whether I could live like Moses, David, and Paul. Also, I asked myself: Should I be a historian? A mathematics scholar? As I agonized over this during the dream-filled years of senior high school, I resolved to study theology. In the background was God's sovereignty; my parents had planned to dedicate their first son to the Lord when they married, and their prayers until they went to heaven greatly influenced me. After taking the road of theology, I faced others choices: Should I be a theologian? A missionary? A pastor? Realizing that the central road of theology is ministry, I chose the road of ministry.

The path of ministry turned out to be near yet far. It was a life where joy, anger, sorrow and pleasure converged. It was a sequence of life that could not be endured without singing songs. In the path of ministry where I wanted to live my whole life with Jesus according to the Word, the songs that God stirred in me were a source of strength and encouragement. Seoul's Suh Moon Church and the First Korean Presbyterian Church of Philadelphia, two churches where I have served as the Senior Pastor, proved to be pastures so suitable for singing songs. I loved the flock of sheep there, still love them, and will continue to love them. It is a joy of the shepherd boy that there is a flock of sheep who will always listen to his songs. And my family, who insists that my songs are the best, are my precious gifts from God.

As I want to share my poems with pastors ministering in America (and around the world) and with saints dedicating themselves for the Kingdom of Christ, I am putting a second volume of poetry (in English) into print. It is my sincere desire that all the pastors serving Christ's Kingdom with me will sing more splendid songs than mine. I give thanks to our Savior, the Triune God. To the saints, the alumni of the Student For Christ movement, fellow ministering workers and family, I offer my deep gratitude.

Rev. Manwoo A. Kim
Philadelphia
May 27, 2003
On our 34th Wedding Anniversary

Acknolwedgement

In publishing this book, I have many to thank. I give thanks, praise, and glory to the Triune God for saving me, who has so many faults, for making me a pastor, for using me for His Kingdom all my life, and for always providing a wealth of emotions to write poetry. I am thankful for the saints and fellow workers at the First Korean Presbyterian Church, who have supported and worked with me as I serve as the Senior Pastor, and for the Student For Christ (SFC) alumni who have always supported me in the work of world missions and in the SFC movement. I would also like to thank my beloved children, Heerak Christian, Youngsun Victoria and Onyoo Elizabeth, who encouraged me to write and publish my poems. And I would like to express my deep appreciation to my lovely wife Sooeun, my lifetime companion, who has served the church together with me and helped me with prayer and encouragement.

"April Is"
(April 21, 2002)

April is
When buddies gather together
Longing for days long ago
A month for singing about the natural grace
Given by God the Creator

Even if
As shadows of times past
On a very clear face is an umbra growing
In Christ friendship inscribed in the heart
Unchanged will shine the light

Because He is our pal
Who did not spare His life but wholly poured out
His blood until the very last one drop
Jesus
Covenant made in His blood will constant be

Within the chorus sung as alumni of heaven
The friendship flowing
The more we sing, the closer in camaraderie we become
The more we hear, the more solid we develop
Joy will overflowing be

Love will abundant be
Buddies of childhood! Pals of youth!
Friends of adulthood!
To the green field of April shining
With glorious light come out hand in hand

Let us offer praise to the Savior of the resurrection
Affection will deepen, trust strengthen
The pulse of eternal life will be felt
The chorus of April sung sitting around the Beloved Shepherd
Will make the First Pasture like the Kingdom of God

April is
When affectionate buddies gather together
A month for singing about the special grace
Given to us by God the Creator
Happy and blessed are we

New Morning of the Pasture

"Building The Church"
(April 28, 2002)

We thank God for His grace.
Today, we have a combined Korean and African-American worship service. All the saints of our congregation, please join in the worship service. Please warmly welcome the Camphor church believers who will be coming to our church, and greet them with kindness.

Next Lord's Day is our Spring Revival weekend.
In Sunday School, Ms. Lorraine Davis, along with two other people, will come and spread God's Word to Sunday School students. In the CEM*, Daniel Pyon JDSN** will preach. Through Pyon JDSN, whose love for the young souls is ardent, our youths' souls will be revived. For the Young Adults Revival, Rev. Shin-gu Lee will give us God's message. As one of the leaders of our Koshin Presbyterian denomination, he has a passionate faith and deep understanding of the Scriptures. He will be an instrument of God's shower of blessing. We will experience the phenomenon of our young adults becoming like the dew of early morning who will gladly dedicate themselves in the church of the Lord.

We will be offering our construction offering on the first Lord's Day of May. Since 1980 the construction offering was collected during every spring's Young Adults Revival. Through continual construction offering, church building construction has been successful thus far. Construction offering collected this year will be used for the first overall repair of the church building since our purchase 18 years ago. It will include the repair of areas that have not passed the test required by the insurance company. You can give the construction offerings in following the ways:

(1) If the amount you promised earlier is still remaining, you may make this offering to pay off that promised amount. You can find out about your amount still outstanding by asking.
(2) For those of you who have already completed paying off the promised amount, you may make a new promise and make an offering toward that amount.

---

* CEM is a shorthand for Covenant English Ministry, the English ministry branch of the First Pasture (*ie.*, First Korean Presbyterian Church of Philadelphia).
** JDSN stands for the Korean title "Jun-Do-Sa-Nim," translated "evangelist." JDSN is under care of the Christian denomination through which ordination is being sought. Normally, JDSN is studying for a Master of Divinity degree at a Christian seminary.

(3) You can pay towards the promised offering over a year or pay every week according to your own schedules of payment and circumstances.
(4) When you give the offering toward the promised amount, please use the construction offering envelopes.
(5) For those saints who have never promised an amount for the construction offering, you may use this opportunity to participate in the work of the church building construction.
(6) I believe that for the believers who give the construction offerings will receive an abundance of spiritual and physical blessings in their personal and family lives, as promised in the Scriptures.

Through the prophet Haggai, God declared that His blessings and grace will surely be upon the saints participating in the work of church building construction.

I pray that upon the saints who always exert their strength for the work of the Lord, the grace and blessing of the Lord will overflow.

"Go up into the mountains and bring down timber and build the house, so that I may take pleasure in it and be honored,' says the LORD" (Haggai 1:8).

New Morning of the Pasture

*"We in Christ"**
(April 28, 2002)

We in Christ
Brothers and sisters
People loved by God
People who love God
Heavenly colleagues

Today
A bright spring day
Let us hand in hand
To the dandelion-blooming green field hasten
And greet the Beloved Shepherd running toward us

For us
He who on the cross shed His blood
Died, was buried, rose again, and ascended
Today on the right hand of God for us prays
Our Savior Jesus Christ
The one and only begotten Son of God

For the past one year
Faces unforgotten
Names unforgettable no matter what
Within prayer remembered
Within remembrance prayed, saints we are glad to meet

With the love of the cross
We love you
In the Word
We respect you
By the inspiration of the Holy Spirit
We greet you

Today we
Through the combined worship
For the living and powerful Father God
Wholeheartedly praise with all our heart
With all our minds
With all our strength give glory
In Christ may our friendship be more solidly kept

---

* This poem was written for the 14th annual combined worship service with fellow African-American brothers and sisters in the Camphor Memorial United Methodist Church.

Manwoo A. Kim

"On Children's Lord's Day"*
(May 5, 2002)

On the hill of Mt. Tabor**
That which the Beloved Shepherd cultivates
First Garden's bluish-green pasture
Like the new buds there
Children of Jesus!

In the new morning dawning
As if shy
Like the dew drops
Hanging on the new buds
Children of Jesus!

Receiving the morning's sunrays
Showing their faces on the mountain far away
Shimmering brilliantly by the drops of dew
Like faces round
Children of Jesus!

High and blue like the sky
Wide and blue like the ocean
Deep and blue like the forest
As the barley grows quickly by the spring wind
As the tree leaflets blossom fully by the balmy breeze

Like lilac, poulownia, wisteria and jasmine
Blooming like the violets of May
In Jesus
Healthily
Prudently

In faith grow
To move the world
Transform history
And offer the earth
On the altar of the Lord

New Morning of the Pasture

Children of Jesus!
In this land
Let the season of Jesus come
Evermore
In the Lord may you happy and blessed be

---

* May 5 is Children's Day in Korea
** The First Pasture (The First Korean Presbyterian Church of Philadelphia) is located on Tabor Road, between 7th and 8th Streets in Philadelphia, PA. The site of the church building is at the end of a long driveway and on a slight elevation. Mt. Tabor is a mountain mentioned in the Bible.

Manwoo A. Kim

"Mother's Day Poem"
(May 12, 2002)

Mother
My and your mother, our mother
Mother of faith

Like Hannah
In order to receive a child of faith
Like Rebekah
In order to have her child of faith receive blessing
Like the wise woman before the court of Solomon
In order to save the child of faith
Like Lois and Eunice
In order to bring up a child of faith
Like the mothers
Embracing their children of faith within their bosom
And coming to Jesus
Regardless of the disciples' preventions
In order that their children might meet Jesus
Like Mary
In order to stand near her suffering son
Not sleeping
Not resting
Not eating
Day and night at all times praying
Mother of love

Mothers, the First Garden's pride
For a long time
Only looking to the promises of the Lord
Rooting out weeds
Pulling out bad shrubs
Scattering seed
Giving water and adding fertilizer
Going to and out of the kitchen
And putting hands inside filthy water
In their table-service
In order to transform the Garden
Into the pasture of the beloved Shepherd
Cultivating the field till hands and feet wear out
Spilling tears of blood and sweat, crying out
Teaching God's word and praying
Mothers of hope

New Morning of the Pasture

On Mother's Day
For giving us the mothers of faith, hope and love
Thanks be to God the Father Almighty

Someday
Children who have grown in the Lord
In good health and wisdom
Will spread out all over the world
And to the living
Powerful God the Father will give limitless glory
The day of great service will surely come

Pour down Your abundant favor
Upon the mothers of the First Garden
May they receive obedience and honor
In the remaining days of their lives
And may comfort overflow
To the right hand of the Father God Almighty who loves
I commit them

Manwoo A. Kim

"Thanks Be To God"
(May 19, 2002)

Thanks be to God for His grace.
We thank Him for saving us, forgiving our sins, making us His children, giving us everlasting life, and making us heirs of eternal heaven. We thank Him for providing us with a church so that we may live a spiritual life on this earth until we go to His Kingdom, receive training as the people of Heaven, and live the life of sanctification. We thank Him for using our church in the past years and enabling us to serve for His glory. We thank Him for providing our church with faithful Kingdom workers.

We thank Him for enabling us to purchase the present church building on June 30, 1986, to dedicate the church building after a seven-year period of the renovation process, and to worship Him, the living and powerful Father God, in this place. We thank Him when we see children born in our church finish school, get married, become workers of church and society, and spread out here and there.

In order that our place of worship, the church building, may be more apt for worship, there is an area of our church that needs renovation. That is the roof. For this repair work the whole church congregation has been praying for the past three years and has been presenting offerings. Now we have arrived at the stage to take the initiative for repair.

After much praying and studying, the Building Committee and the Session of Elders have come to the conclusion that it is reasonable and agreeable for us to use our own hands to renovate our beloved church of the Lord with good materials purchased for the purpose. Our personal involvement will be glorifying to the Lord Jesus.

Although every Memorial Day we normally go for an outdoor church picnic, this year all the church members will gather together at church. Sunday School, Youth Group, College Group, and Senior Citizens Group will pass an enjoyable time on the church grass, while the Young Adults Group, Men's and Women's Evangelical Groups, and Adults' Evangelical Group will exert their efforts to dedicate and serve in the work of roof repair. Women's Evangelical Groups will prepare tasty and nutritional food of high culinary quality. After finishing the work of roof repair, Young Adults, Evangelical Groups and Adults' Group will join in joyous fellowship.

New Morning of the Pasture

I know that we will relish the joy of having killed "two birds with one stone" during this year's outdoor church picnic in the church compound as we make the Memorial Day a day of mobilization for church service and beautification of our faith's site.

I am thankful for the service of love of the believers, the dear people of God, who are always diligent in the work of the Lord. I pray that the joy of full participation in the work of Christ's church will be abundant.

Manwoo A. Kim

"The Memorial Day"
(May 26, 2002)

People who live for their country
Who die for their country

In the bosoms of how many people
Must have they instilled peace
In the bosoms of how many people
Must have they hammered a nail
In the bosoms of how many people
Must have they caused a river of tears to flow

When the dandelions have bloomed
And white roses are hanging here and there in clusters
In a rosary
While violet paulownia flowers are starting to fall
People who bring thoughts to mind
Soldiers whose names one might not know

Death in the line of duty
Dying for one's country
Martyrdom

When the sound of a cuckoo
Weaving through the wheat field
Heard, riding the wind of spring
Is ringing the eardrums
Hill mountain neighborhood
Widowed mother who lost her son
Fruit merchant's wife who lost her husband
Orphaned brothers and sisters who lost their father
In grief are tearing

Longing belongs to us all
Memories, after stopping by the lilac-blossoming hill
Like a stork flying
Flapping over a zelkova tree on the outskirts of the village
Recollections scattered haphazardly
Over the places brushed by war
And there letting bloom forget-me-not's

New Morning of the Pasture

While proclaiming the good news of the Kingdom of God
People who have poured down their lives and have gone
People who died but will rise again
Until far away in the future we meet in that Land
In our bosoms the river water of longing will ceaselessly flow

Manwoo A. Kim

"In The First Garden's Hillside"
(June 2, 2002)

In the First Garden's hillside
Let us plant several more Canadian maple trees
In the midst of the greenish pasture
Make a little stream and let clear water flow
Through four-season cycles

When scorching sunrays of high noon are intense
Where heat-consumed spirits can find their way here
And lay their bodies down comfortably
To fully quench their parched throats
Let us make it a resting place of peace

High summer
That even the Beloved Shepherd is seeking
When the mountain birds are chirping
Where gentle breeze
Deep with sweet pine-fragrance blows
To cool off His forehead's sweat
Formed from saving souls
Let us make it a dwelling place of love

Where in the corrupted world
Stung by the poison of libertine culture
Minds becoming ever more desiccated
Hearts roughened
Even personalities emitting stench
Can become spotlessly purified
Made into a temple
Where the Holy Spirit can reside
Let us cultivate it into a spiritual location of repose

We are all together strangers
Heaven-bound pilgrims
Where those lonely and sad
In agony or in pain
Even when abandoned
After having failed and in despair
With no way out
Can dart toward the green pastures

New Morning of the Pasture

Beside the quiet waters
And lay their bodies down
Look up at the white clouds
Floating across the blue sky
And open wide the doors of their hearts
To the living, powerful Father God
Let us make it a garden
Where they await a new morning of hope

There will be thanksgiving, praise
And joy overflow always

Manwoo A. Kim

"Wilderness Of The Middle East"
(June 9, 2002)

Wilderness of the Middle East
Barren land
Desert region
Fluctuating between 40 and 50 degrees Celsius
Heat zone
Where going barefoot would but infallibly scald
Even there
One lonesome Shittim tree stands erect
Protruding greenish leaves
Blooming flowers
Bearing fruit
Because from the depths of the earth
Roots lowered
Reached the source of subterranean water

Though the sandy *terra firma*
From any angle
Reveals not an iota of moisture
In the area of Palestine
Where groves of dates and coconut grow thick
Those dreaming the visions of Isaiah the prophet
Sprinkle water drawn up from the heart of the earth
Thus primary-colored posies of strong fragrance
Gorgeously blossom
Dates and coconuts in clusters
Appearing and awaiting the time of harvest

By libertine civilization
Dilapidating mentality culture
Hearts like burning grains of sand
Knitting together a criminal society
From violence, murder, depravity
War tainting villages of the globe
Even there
If the river of life flowed good soil will they be
If blessed seasonal rain fell forest in full will grow

New Morning of the Pasture

Though a life deserving only death
From original and actual sin
If not trusting in man
Not treating flesh and blood as power
Not forsaking the Lord
But on the Lord of faith
Jesus the river of life
Trusting and depending
Like a tree planted by streams of water
Will extend its roots by the riverside
Through the fire's heat will not fear
Though a drought suddenly befell
Its leaves verdant
In season will yield fruit

In the First Pasture
Fenced in from the desert-like wilderness
River of life always flows for the flock of sheep
To dampen their throats
Leafy shade grows luxuriant
That beautiful birds' chirping never ceases
Flowers bloom, fruits hang
In a well-watered garden
Being made by the beloved Shepherd
Our souls' really awesome gardener He is
How very blessed we are

Manwoo A. Kim

"The Lord Will Provide"
(June 16, 2002)

As mid-summer tree leaves turn greener
If only our hearts like the heart of Jesus
By His wonderful grace
Without one blemish
Became more verdant

Like fluffy, cottony clouds
Floating high in the sky
If only with hopes, dreams
Ideals, aspirations and desires
Fully loaded
Our hearts like the heart of Jesus
By the precious blood of the cross
Increasingly became whiter
Much whiter

Wider than the ocean
Grace abounding, the love of the cross
If only over sands splashing a spray of water
With waves come crashing
Soaked our parched bosoms

If only the aroma of Christ
Like the fragrance of a wild briar rose
Whenever the hot winds blew
Spread through suffocating stench-filled back city alleys
And souls smothered were revived

If only when souls once lonely and wandering
On the holy Lord's Day morning
Came upon and entered the First Pasture
The beloved Shepherd's voice that renews
Brimfully overflowed every bosom
Receiving new strength
In faith, hope and love
To the living Father God
We're able to offer sincere worship

New Morning of the Pasture

The longing of the saints in Christ
A reality to be fulfilled
On the day of Jesus Christ

Like the high summer's gentle breeze
Grazing the collars
If only deep into the heat-consumed spirits
The Holy Spirit's gusts blew
Withered souls received new strength
And the joy of the dear people
Diligent in the work of the Lord flowed over

The Lord will provide

Manwoo A. Kim

"A Bird Without Wings"
(June 23, 2002)

A bird without wings
Though with wings a bird that cannot fly is not a bird
Even if it wants to fly
A bird without wings is a bird that cannot fly
On the grass crouching
Soothing loneliness
Still awaiting that day of flight
It nurtures the dream of the blue sky

There will be a day when the wings will grow
A day when new strength will be provided to the wings
It will but fly
Through one section of that bluish expanse
It will fly as much as it wants

Over that far away river flowing
Lake sparkling by afternoon sunrays
Forest thickened
Hill fully blossoming with wild chrysanthemums
Line of cars hastening on the highways
A little kid going to the church
Hand in hand with mom and dad
Person straining and driving his wheelchair
Field of roses
Farmer pouring marble sweat
Even the flock of sheep over the pasture
Blooming white with clovers

Welcoming and looking up to the beloved Shepherd
Searching for the First Pasture
If to the voice of Truth it gears its ears
It inscribes in the tablets of its heart
Believes and follows
Wings will sprout
Receiving renewed strength
Like eagles will be able to fly

New Morning of the Pasture

Fly
Making way through the clouds
Soar
High, high
Even higher to the throne of heaven
With faith on wings
Far, far away
Fly

Riding the chariots of fire, the horses of fire
Like Elijah in a whirl
Flying up toward the new heaven and the new earth
By the river of the water of life it will arrive

Until the new morning comes
In the Lord with wings spread out
Soar
Through Him who gives me strength
If wanting to fly
I will but fly

Manwoo A. Kim

"Do You Believe In Hell?"
(June 30, 2002)

Do you believe in hell?
You
Clothed with the beloved Shepherd's favor
Do you believe in the final judgment?

Not thinking about the autumn harvest
And scattering the seed
There would be no such farmer

Though expecting grain while scattering seed
At the time of the harvest chaff will appear
Which the wind blows away
In the harvest will be burned

If to pulverized soil magnet is placed
Adhering metal pieces will be taken away
While the remaining soil will be but forsaken
Like so
In that last day of judgment human existence also
To life or death will be separated

Road of belief, road of unbelief
Way of the sinner, path of the righteous
Track of the evil, trail of the good
According to the road of blessing or of woe
Traversed humanity will be spilt apart
Is it heaven-bound or hell-bound?

Those who believe in the Son of God
The Lord Jesus Christ as Savior
And obey God's Word
On that day will be approved
Those walking in the counsel of the wicked
Standing in the way of sinners
Sitting in the seat of mockers
And in unbelief disobeying
Will not be able to enter the assembly of the righteous
Will be chased away

New Morning of the Pasture

Hell
Where burning sulfur blazes up in flames
Homeland of tragedy
Location of utmost misery
Where all attempts to die will prove fruitless
Place of torment where the rich man squirmed
And asked for a tiny gulp of water
Filled with darkness, grief and curse
Where the devils enter
So scary and fearful that they wince
To that fire of hell they will enter

Saints
Who have been saved
Must not slow their footsteps
Toward the heavenly city
But run pressing on
Hell left behind
Forward
Forward to the new heaven and new earth
Forward

Manwoo A. Kim

"Have You Heard?"
(July 7, 2002)

Have you heard?
Have you given ear?
Have you had concerns?
Have you listened?

To the sounds from hell

To the crying out
"Dip your hand with a drop of water and
Soak the scorched throat
Dried lips
Thirst-filled tongue"
Feeling the lack of a gulp of water

To the sorrowful sounds of that person so arrogant
So self-confident
So living well, faring richly
So apathetic
So shunning the beggar filled with suffering
So thoroughly unbelieving

To the shameless sounds begging
"Dip your finger tip in the water and cool my tongue"
Without self-pride, face-saving, or dignity
Using the person he had once despised
Treated contemptuously
Abused

To the moaning sounds
"Tell the tragic news of hell
To the people who cannot but come into hell"
That they not come into hell
People like himself not believing
Not bestowing love
Belittling God
Among his parents, brothers and sisters
On earth

New Morning of the Pasture

Hell is such a place
For person who went to hell
Or person who had not been to hell
Or person who will go to hell
A place each and everyone hates
And trembles at from fear
Ghastly destination full of lamentation
Regret, sorrow
Pain, thirst and starvation
Resentment and judgment

Oh what of this?
If not listening to the Law and the Prophets
If not believing God's Word
Inspired by the Holy Spirit
If rejecting the Gospel of heaven and hell
If not obeying the Word of Truth
And so if cannot believe Lord Jesus Christ
The Son of God as Savior
Denying faith though knowing
From hearing and learning about Jesus
And even after tasting the spiritual grace
That they will only enter
This grim reality

Manwoo A. Kim

"In The Summer Plants Grow"
(July 14, 2002)

In the summer
Though the sweltering heat and humidity irritate
Plants grow
To provide benefit

Rainstorm raging, tempest blasting
Trees cut down
Though the seas seem to overturn in whole
To cleanse all kinds of garbage
That has flowed into the ocean
It is necessary

Farmer, even though the sunrays are stinging so
In the paddy fields weeds
Carpenter vigorously nails
Traffic police standing on one side of the road
Keeps traffic control

Students attending summer school
Though the mountain-field wind is blowing
Forest-thickened park is nearby
Though the blue ocean
With white sand and cool breeze blowing beckons
Without a stare, go to class

Heavenly citizens, God's sons and daughters!
The First Church's saved believers
To a place we hasten whenever summer arrives
The Pocono's retreat center
Where there is the Word of Truth
Praises glorifying God
Passionate prayer
Fellowship of the saints
Earnest Bible-memorizing
Spiritual banquet for us only
The church-wide summer retreat
To the seat making more yearning memories
With the passing of days
Gather with all effort

New Morning of the Pasture

Beloved brothers and sisters
This year also mutually embracing
The heart-rending love of Christ in our bosoms
Congregating and to the beautiful stories of heaven
Gearing ears
In the joy of being made one in Christ will you not share?

Let us all together at the Pocono's retreat center meet

Manwoo A. Kim

"Heart That Yearns After Grace"
(July 21, 2002)

Heart that yearns after grace
Is a beautiful thing
A good heart given by the Shepherd of Love

The more one longs for grace
The more will one acquire spiritual competency
Nearer to God he will draw

Though wanting to share
Desiring to be a Good Samaritan
Wishing to be a warm neighbor to those in need of help
Without love he will not be able

Without the love of the cross
Speaking in the tongues of angels
Will yield a sound of clanging cymbals
As if on ground that is futile
And darkness that is deep
An empty existence it will merely become

To not live in vain
To be a life bearing fruit
To transmit spiritual inheritance
To generations coming in succession
A believer kicks and struggles

Upon hearing the Word, life overflows
When singing praise, peace inundates
In the time of praying, joy runs over

That is why
We go
To meet at the Pocono's Retreat Center
To listen to the loving voice of the Beloved Shepherd
Hastening toward us
We go to the church-wide summer conference

The heavenly banquet of the dear heavenly people
On top of the mountain
Every year
Renews our souls

"Prayer Support"
(July 28, 2002)

Thanks be unto God for His grace.
From Tuesday to Friday, the Second National Conference of SFC in America will be held at Villanova University. Prior to and following the conference many visitors will be coming to our church. We need to provide food, lodging and convenient transportation for them. Above all, we need to be courteous to them. We need to let them feel Christ's love of the cross. During the conference, we need to give much glory to God. The speakers must proclaim God's word fearlessly. The students must receive the fullness of the Holy Spirit and work out campus evangelization in America. We also need clear and cool weather. God has to fill the necessary expenses of the conference. Villanova University authorities have to be gracious to the students, so that there will be no hindrance in receiving grace. All the people serving for the conference have to serve with joy and thankfulness. People from out of the country have to arrive safely. I look forward to the heavenly blessings that will be abundant upon our SFC alumni.

For all these topics, I especially request your prayers during this week. Let us pray that the campuses will be evangelized, that American students will return to Jesus Christ, and that American churches will return to the Bible. Let us pray that the Gospel will spread and Reformed churches will be established in America. The prayer of the saints in faith will be powerful and effective. As answer to our prayers, may this conference be full of grace. Through this national SFC conference, I am confident that God's will will be done on this American land as in heaven. I believe that the SFC movement in America will be a fun faith movement in Christ.

Once again, I ask you for your prayer support.

Manwoo A. Kim

"A Word of Welcome"
(July 30, 2002)

Hallelujah! Praise be to God's holy name.

The Student For Christ movement (SFC), which started in Korea 55 years ago, had its first conference in America (in Philadelphia) in August of 1979. Since then, SFC has spread out to the East Coast, the West Coast, the Northwest, and the Mid-south of the United States, as well as to Canada and South America. SFC holds a conference every summer and one every winter, and campus evangelization has continued in various colleges. In Los Angeles in 1998, commemorating the 20th anniversary of SFC in America, we held the First National Conference with about 1050 people in attendance. This time again we have gathered with about 1000 students and have opened the Second National Conference. Over the years, about 20,000 youths have received spiritual training and are now vibrantly active as heavenly workers in the mainstream American society. We give thanks, praise and glory to the living God.

In their First National Conference, SFC students from Argentina recited the SFC principles in Spanish, which was a first in the history of SFC. This year's Second National Conference has an international character, with people from the USA, Korea, Canada, Brazil, Argentina, Paraguay, Peru, Puerto Rico, Sierra Leon in Africa, China, and elsewhere.

This year, receiving the fullness of the Holy Spirit and God's Word, with Reformed faith that is God-centered, Bible-centered, and church-centered, we should use this opportunity for campus and world evangelization.

In the name of the Lord Jesus Christ, we welcome all of you participating in this conference. We sincerely thank the churches and believers as well as the SFC alumni who have supported this conference with prayer, service and financial contributions. Even if there is some inconvenience, please bear with us in the love of Christ.

I wish that you will meet a new turning point in your scholarship, faith and life. I believe that God the Father will surely bless you. Thank the Lord.

New Morning of the Pasture

"Being confident of this, that he who began a good work in you will carry it on to completion until the day of Christ Jesus" (Philippians 1:6). Amen.

In Christ,

Rev. Manwoo A. Kim
Supervisory Chairman
Student For Christ in America
Second National Conference

Manwoo A. Kim

"Student For Christ"
(August 2, 2002)

That day
The sky over Villanova University was so blue

Like canna flowers
Faces fully blooming
Bodies heated by the Spirit's fire
Hotter than the heat of the summer

Not drifting away
With wild waves of libertine culture
Not drowning in the corrupt campus climate
Resisting the prodigal lifestyles of peers
Forms faithful, having hastened to the garden of grace
Because the highway of Zion was in their hearts

When listening to the Word of Truth
Like the stars of the night sky
Eye-light shining twinkle, twinkle
Within was a reflection of Jesus

When praising with hands clapping and voices raised
It was as if the axis of earth was shaking
Like the fierce wave beating upon the shore
As if lightening, thunder and rain were pouring down
The Holy Spirit's inspiration, a work of grace

As the Red Sea split asunder and a way appeared
Rock burst and a spring flowed
Like the desert changed to a fertile land
There the renewed spirits were
To the glory of God

Embracing within the principles of life
God-centered, Bible-centered, church-centered
Becoming the mind, heart and fragrance of Jesus
Returning to their families, churches and campuses
Students of the Student For Christ
How they resembled the image of Jesus

New Morning of the Pasture

Like the dark hue of canna flowers
Planted in the inner court of God's field
Burning bosoms
When autumn comes
Will harvest 12 basketfuls of the fruits
Of campus evangelism
Thanksgiving and praise will overflow
Hallelujah, amen.

Manwoo A. Kim

"Let Us Exalt God's Holy Name"
(August 4, 2002)

Hallelujah! Let us exalt God's holy name.
We thank God for His grace. The blessings which the living and powerful God has bestowed upon us in this Second National Student for Christ conference in America are innumerable. Amid the continual heat wave and thunderstorm forecasts, it was hard to picture how we could serve the students gathering like bees from all directions. We were uncertain of the security of our enormous budget and the effective implementation of our immense number of programs.

So we could only pray. From two months prior we sent prayer topics to all the member churches in America and in two stages continually prayed for the topics. From our church members we requested continual prayer support daily for one month. Every early rise morning we cried out and sincerely asked others to pray for us. Every Thursday at 10 am, the SFC preparation committee members gathered in the church and continually prayed. We could only trust and pray. (During the preparations, two directors had to be admitted to the emergency room from exhaustion and a car accident!) We sent 2000 donation letters. It was a preparation stage where everything appeared sloppy and lacking, but God worked in His sovereignty for His kingdom and His righteousness. I will not be able to write all the thank you's, but I would like to offer glory to God with the following few.
1) For giving us a clear, nice, and increasingly cooler weather
2) For 1300 attendees every evening and a registration of 900
3) For sufficiently filling up our budget
4) For the sacrificial faithfulness of the directors and staff
5) For Villanova University's graciousness, good environment, tasty meals
6) For the speakers' messages consistent with the Reformed faith
7) For the smooth running of the programs and cooperation of the students
8) For safe entry into this country from Korea and other countries
9) For watching over our transportation
10) For the prayer and financial support of our denomination churches
11) For the active and constructive participation of our denomination pastors
12) For our church members' sweat of joy and hand service of dedication

New Morning of the Pasture

There are many more topics of thanksgiving. I am convinced that the students who have received grace and blessing will now return to their churches, homes, and campuses and arise and shine. This fall, campus evangelization will see great growth. In the next ten years SFC conferences will meet in different parts of the world. We give glory to God.

May the creation blessings of the God the Lord of Creation be abundant upon all the saints of our church who have worked hard so that tomorrow's church workers will spread the holy Reformed faith movement all over the world.

Thank you.

Manwoo A. Kim

"Like Farmers Over-Anxious"
(August 11, 2002)

Like farmers over-anxious
Because not even a handful of raindrop falls
Upon the grains burning up with thirst
In the open field where summer is passing through

Even when parched spirits
Are disappointed
Because there is no sweet rain that soaks
Despite waiting in expectation of God's merciful hand
And crying out

The living, powerful Father God
As always looks down upon us
To those who believe that He neither sleeps nor slumbers
But is there watching over us
Will there be hope

The loving Lord demanding faith from us
Says
Commit to me
Trust me
Believe me
Ask, seek, knock
Be still and see God's salvation

Even in the thick darkness stars shine
Inside a tempest
Behind the black cloud
The sun is illuminating
To those who know
That even in the Red Sea was once a road
There will be no despair

Raising the weak
The dull-witted, the dense
The foolish, the lowly
Shaming the strong
The prudent, the savvy
The wise, the famous
The Creator God is so good

New Morning of the Pasture

The road of life is not with human beings
Walking the steps is not with pedestrians
Believing that it is up to the One who enables the walking
Trusting that in due time He will fulfill
And not giving up while doing the good work
To those awaiting the time and praying
Always will come a new morning
When the bright sun widely smiles

Manwoo A. Kim

"Night When Star Is Shining"
(August 25, 2002)

Night when star is shining
During the night when starlight is awesomely splendid
The night when the Chesapeake Bay salty sea wind
Cools the poured sweat of high noon
Gathered, adoring grace
Daughters of Zion, into whose hearts blows
The fire of the Holy Spirit

When the Word of Truth
Like serene waves
Washes up on the seashore
In darkness star shines even brighter
As blackness deepens the starlight that twinkles more
Though the thunderstorm comes pushing hard
Behind the black cloud always shines
Even from hundreds of light years away
Arrives to a small place in the corner of the earth
Without a speck of shame, showing brilliance -
The bright Morning Star

In Christ so happy, so joyful
Praising God all night long, the daughters of God
With cries
Exhaustion cannot overcome and alert through the night
The sisters of heaven
Beloved children
They call out in name one by one and pray
The mothers of faith
For the construction of God's kingdom
With burning bosoms
Following the voice of the Beloved Shepherd
Faithful to His promises
And hastening
White sheep so pure, so innocent
From eyes letting countless tear drops fall
The women-servants of the Lord
First Korean Presbyterian Church of Philadelphia's
Christian women of faith
The testimony of service, the praise of lips

New Morning of the Pasture

The strength of prayer, listening ears
A reflection of heaven's luminosity in their eyes
Blessed women saints of Jerusalem
The bride of Christ
Precious members of the Women's Evangelical Groups
In their hearts will It shine

When in the path of the pasture darkness settles
On the lonesome evening road of return
From shepherding scattered flock of sheep
Because from an unfathomable far away distance
There is Star shining on this land
The shepherd-boy is not lonely
Closing the door of the sheep pen of the cuddly flock
Appreciating the evening symphony
A medley of anonymous grass insects
And the resonance of waves caressing the sand
For the Star poured down on the surface of the water
To evermore shine in the hearts of the daughters of faith
With the Shepherd of Love
To shower great grace
Through the deep of the night
Do I plead and plead

* Following the 11th Women's Evangelical Group Conference

Manwoo A. Kim

"Autumnaf Fragrance Permeates"
(September 1, 2002)

Summer of grace has passed
And already
Autumnal fragrance permeates

Betwixt branches
Checking the leaves
Looking to find fruit, hand trembles

How much
How big
How lovely, scrumptious, aromatic
How solidly have hung fruits?

The more hand fumbles through
Not one comes within grasp and so heart is empty
Soon the master of the orchard will return
What to do?

The pitiable keeper of the orchard
With face blushing and head bowed
Will utter his voice feeble as the sound of mosquitoes

"Be patient for just one more year
I will dig deep, give fertilizer and tend
Next fall there will surely be fruit"

Every fall a repeated confession
Whenever autumn arrives
A story told innumerable times
Without becoming angry
Beamingly smiling and lending ear
So good, the Shepherd of Love
Before Him
An oft-falling existence not giving up
Not discouraged even in the hollow autumn
Once again tending to the branches
Tilling the field, giving fertilizer
Longing for the coming bountiful fall
Will cultivate trees of dream

New Morning of the Pasture

A prayer offered in the deepening fall
"Be patient for just one more time and please wait!"
A heart awaiting autumn again
The heart of the orchard keeper

Manwoo A. Kim

"Autumn Is A Going Away Season"
(September 8, 2002)

Autumn is a going away season
Treasured children grow
Leave their mom and dad's bosoms
Depart from their affectionate church

To a place under higher skies
Toward a wider world
Where there is teaching, learning and realizing
Where tomorrow is designed
Once they leave for the public place
Where here and there gathered human families
Put their heads together and research
Empty heart, hollow fall
Because my one year has just passed
Heart breaks

So profound, not easily understood
God's sovereignty, providence, will

But one thing is sure
In all things
God will work for the good of those who love Him
Who have been called according to His purpose
So why be saddened?
I will commit, pray, place my hope, trust

Still under the shade of a big armful of tree
In the First Pasture
As if feeling something is missing
With the summer's exit
As if the approaching autumn is merry
Are the sounds of cicada crying
Singing that the learners flittering away
And disappearing somewhere
In forms recognizable within the flow of times
Some day in this land we will encounter
Shouting that some day in the heavens
We will meet face to face

New Morning of the Pasture

Because always living deep within the bosom
Thanksgiving overflows
Whenever nurturing memories of the children of God
Workers of heaven of the First Pasture
People of Jesus
Within reminiscence smiling
And within prayer unforgotten
Will come to mind

As for the saints who are in the land
They are the glorious ones in whom is all my delight
Though departure is sorrowful
Truly precious and pride-worthy are they

Manwoo A. Kim

"With Autumn's Drizzle Descending"
(September 15, 2002)

With autumn's drizzle descending
When rain dampened leaves fall rustling
To the beloved Shepherd
Looking for fruit trees in the First Pasture
What kind of fruit shall I offer?

Fruits of love, joy, peace, patience
Kindness, goodness, faithfulness
Gentleness, self-control, poverty of spirit, mournfulness
Thirsting and hungering after righteousness
Mercy, purity, peace, righteousness, truth
Holiness, faith, virtue, knowledge, wisdom
Godliness, brotherly kindness, hope and long-suffering
Not fruits of bitter envy, boasting, rudeness
Self-seeking, being angry, evil deeds
Unrighteousness, hatred, envy, jealousy, doubt
Complaining, fighting, impurity and deceit

Because sparse, unripe, not well-grown
It is embarrassing to put forward
And face reddens

Full of love, kindness, benevolence and mercy
Not ashamed of us who are weak
Lowly and repeatedly failing
Because delighting to forgive our sins and transgressions
Throwing afar our sins
Changeless and still, as before treating us
The beloved Shepherd, the Lord Jesus Christ
With whose Father
I shall plead

That it was because of the orchard keeper
Because of a lacking, foolishness, languor, stupidity
I shall cry, weep, repent and confess directly

One more time
To be patient and wait
To not forsake, avoid or forget but show love
As before to come looking to the First Pasture
When the new morning comes to enable fruit-bearing

New Morning of the Pasture

That faithfulness, service, dedication
Exertion of efforts and sacrifice
With pleasure I shall be able to do

Manwoo A. Kim

"The Earth's Axis Slanting"
(September 22, 2002)

The earth's axis slanting
Day shortening, night lengthening
At the autumn's crossroads
Hearts of the First Pasture's sheep flock are busy

For the cold and long winter nights
Will shed and exchange fur
As they graze in the fields to heart's content
Till strength shoot up in the legs

Workers' hands stacking a pile of hay are engaged
On the forehead of the shepherd boy
Pointing to the fold sprouts sweat
When afternoon's languid sunrays
Beat upon the faces of the coloring trees
Standing in rows along the wooden fence
Is the voice of the beloved Shepherd
Who is approaching

Do not let your hearts be troubled
Trust in God, trust also in me

Come to me, all you who are weary and burdened
And I will give you rest

Come, all you who are thirsty, come to the waters
And you who have no money
Come, buy and eat!
Come, buy wine and milk without money
And without cost

In the Pasture dispersing there is peace
In the souls heard there is security
Tranquility of the evening's half-day
Silently growing dark

,Like always
The First Pasture's gathered sheep
For whom the beloved Shepherd comes looking
Will praise

New Morning of the Pasture

The LORD is my shepherd
I shall not be in want

Jesus who for us gave His life is our Good Shepherd

Manwoo A. Kim

"Autumn Rain"
(September 29, 2002)

Autumn rain

On the heart's window
Brushing with the beloved One's beautiful heart
To a rainbow luminosity
Awaking morning's sleep
Knock

Gorgeous brilliancy
Spreads through the bosom in fullness
And to adoring eternity
Forming a melody of happiness
Mystery

During a lifetime
Changeless
Whispering of a delicate sound
A heart-rending affection
From over there in the heavens heard
Music

Reminiscing the past days one by one
Causing saturation in nostalgia
Strength

Drops of blood that dripped from the cross
Falling on the jagged rocks of the hill of Golgotha
Resounding
Love, forgiveness, sound of reconciliation

Autumn rain
On the heart's window brushing
Calling out to the souls
All day long on the First Pasture
Descends gently
Drizzling
Ground is becoming thoroughly soaked

New Morning of the Pasture

"The Heart That Jesus Likes"
(October 6, 2002)

The heart that Jesus likes
A heart of meekness, humility
Sincerity, faithfulness
Heart of Jesus
Heart that loves God with passion
Heart that loves one's neighbor as oneself
Knowing how to sacrifice for righteousness
Truth, and justice
When worshiping the Lord
Pouring out heart like water
Mindset of fighting with sin till bloodshed
Heart mourning and repenting
Honest soul
Biblical conscience of the saved saint

The heart that Jesus dislikes
A lewd, carnal, deceitful, vicious heart
Heart of envy, jealousy, grumbling
Suspicion, and quarreling
Heart trusting in, looking up to
Waiting in expectation of men
Heart of covetousness, avarice
Greed, and idolatry
Fearing, being intimidated by
Being afraid of men and having dread
Mentality of treating the Lord carelessly
Conscience seared as with hot iron
Dirty conscience, shipwrecked conscience
Heart of grudging, revenge
And not knowing forgiveness
Betraying
Insensitive
Ungrateful heart

To become like Jesus
To follow Jesus
While running toward the hill of Golgotha
Collapsing, tripping, falling head down
When wailing, lamenting

Manwoo A. Kim

Crying about and screaming
Comes the voice of the beloved Shepherd
Approaching with a serene smile
I love you
For you I bore the cross
Though you cannot walk in your own strength
I will hold you
Let us walk together
Do not worry, do not fear
Do not be discouraged
Do not be afraid
I do not give up on you
I forgive
Till the end will I look upon you
Will give you a good heart
So that you will arrive at the garden of grace

To rid the heart Jesus dislikes
To have the heart Jesus likes
The flock of sheep running toward the First Pasture
Upon whom with love-filled eyes gazes Jesus
Because He guarantees the end's victory
How thankful
Hallelujah

New Morning of the Pasture

"The Final One Word Spoken"
(October 13, 2002)

The final one word spoken
Voice that comes slicing through the bosom
Sound of love that will raise numerous souls

Go ye into all the world
And preach the Gospel to many nations
You are witnesses of all these things
Go and make disciples of all nations
Baptizing them in the name of the Father
And of the Son and of the Holy Spirit
And teaching them to obey everything
I have commanded you
But you will receive power
When the Holy Spirit comes on you
And you will be my witnesses in Jerusalem
And in all Judea and Samaria
And to the ends of the earth

Do you love me?
Do you truly love me more than these?
Feed my lambs
Take care of my sheep
Follow me

From ears to lips
From lips to ears
From Palestine over the Mediterranean
To Asia Minor
From Asia Minor over Macedonia through Achaia
To Rome
From Europe over the Atlantic Ocean
To America
From America over the Pacific Ocean
To Korea
For 1800 years the Gospel of life
That has been advancing

How many tears must have dropped
How much crying out must there have been

Manwoo A. Kim

How much blood must have been shed
Through countless dedication, sacrifice
Proclamation, missions, martyrdom
Now here even to us the heavenly Gospel
That has swept up in waves cannot be stopped

Whether they listen or fail to listen
In season or out of season
Pathway, rocky places, thorny ground, good soil
Wherever
The Word of Truth that saves soul shall I scatter

Ringing in our ears
Could it not be Jesus' last words of request?

"God The Father's Salvation Plan"
(October 20, 2002)

God the Father's salvation plan
God the Son's plan fruition
God the Holy Spirit's fruition application

By believing
Forgiveness of sins, salvation, regeneration
Being God's child, eternal life, justification
Heirship, one body, process of sanctification
The wondrous grace of the Triune God
How it amazes and demands gratitude

In the seat of daily life
Again and again falling and collapsing
Making mistakes, failing, wavering
Self not being able to do the good desired
And keep on doing evil unwanted
Even in one day a cry shouted several times

What a wretched man I am!
Who will rescue me from this body of death?
Take my life
It is better that I die than live
Though the spirit is willing the body is weak

Still
Waiting, long-suffering
That He is watching and waiting to forgive
Is because of the merit of the precious blood of the cross
His patience till repentance

Whenever receiving the communion
A sense of sin surging up
Heart running toward beneath the cross
On the hill of Golgotha
Spirit wishing to cry out and wail to heart's content
While beating the bosom
A heart that grieves and repents, grant abundantly
Forgive

Manwoo A. Kim

Grace of the forgiveness of sin
Spirit becoming refreshed
Soul lightening
Inner man overflowing with joy

Who can be against us?
Who will bring charge?
Who is he that condemns?
Who shall separate us from the love of the cross?

For all in Christ Jesus
There will never be condemnation
I really like Jesus very much

"Early In The Morning"
(October 27, 2002)

Early in the morning
Heart chilled by autumn's cold rain
Pitiable trees, faces turning yellowish
After fruits have been taken away
Even the empty branches
Unable to soothe loneliness are forlorn
Yet birds that in midsummer so gaily sought them
Where are they wandering about now?

By the fence neatly blooming
The Queen of Fall
Dyed yellow orange white chrysanthemums
Diffusing strong fragrance
More and more seem brightest
Yet do honey bees not flock to them at all?

With the sound of the beloved Shepherd
Knocking on the door
All day long over the field of the First Pasture
Falling rain
Urges the autumn
That is resplendent with variegated colors
Yet are the sheep still lying down

Even on the rainy day
The footsteps of the pilgrim cannot desist
Bedraggled and chilled to the bones, yet
To prepare for winter
Must again erect the wooden fence and handle the pen
Must shout

Awake
Arise
Prepare
Pray without ceasing

Now soon though snow will descend
And season like death freezing over arrives
To the souls not resting

Manwoo A. Kim

From calling on the name of the beloved Shepherd
Even winter, like spring
Will be consistent days of divine favor

Even on the rainy day
Sheep must come out and eat grass to live

"Let Us Wholeheartedly Proclaim"
(November 3, 2002)

God of love
Because God the Lord of Creation
Our Father who dwells in heaven
Is gracious, merciful and loving
To save life dead from sin and transgressions
Sent His One and only begotten Son
Jesus Christ to this earth unsparingly
Had Him suffer the gruesome death of the cross
With flesh torn, blood shed
So that people who believe in Jesus Christ as Savior
From sin and death He delivered
Freed, revived, and saved

God the Father of love
Because He rejoices more
Over one sinner repenting and returning
Than over 99 righteous
And with evangelism
That seems like foolishness to the people of this world
He is pleased to save those who believe
For us of the Reformed faith
Who confess that the chief end of man is to glorify God
And enjoy Him forever
As we pass through the Reformation commemoration day
To the unbelievers
Of over half of the 70,000 fellow brethren in Philadelphia
With all our strength evangelizing
May we know to please God

Whether they listen or fail to listen
In season or out of season
That Jesus Christ is the way
The truth and the life
The Son of God
Who to save us died on the cross and was raised to life
And whoever believes
Will receive forgiveness of sins and will be saved
Let us wholeheartedly proclaim

Woe to me if I don't preach the Gospel
Whoever calls on the name of Jesus Christ
Will not perish but receive salvation.

Manwoo A. Kim

"New Day"
(November 10, 2002)

New day
New morning's sunrays
When
Upon the brilliantly coloring tinged autumnal leaves
They begin to rest
After the end of early rise prayer
Within the saint exiting the door of the church sanctuary
The heart of Jesus
Color of humility, of meekness

As always
Unable to hide even a small speck
Absent-mindedly shedding tears
Clear and lucid souls within
Illumination of the Holy Spirit seeking and coming
Words of truth like morning light
After the retreat of darkness
Are filled to the brim and overflowing

Crimson shade of love
Yellow tint of forgiveness
Color of greyish dark brown of patience

Trees that endured the mid-summer
At the First Garden
Are beautiful in autumn

Robed in the shining garment of glory
The One coming every holy Lord's Day morning
King of kings, the beloved Shepherd
Even He under the trees stands
And gazing at the autumnal leaves
Each showing seasonal tints
Will be pleased

Because life where though the outward man wastes away
The inner man is daily renewed is there
Sparing, embracing, encouraging one another
Will enjoy peace given in the Lord

God's people exiting the sanctuary door at dawn
To the heart of Jesus will prettily be dyed

"Though Having Nothing To Offer"
(November 17, 2002)

Though having nothing to offer
Wishing to give
Looking
Seeking to see if there is anything to present
Heart that is poor
The Lord will see

Though wishing to give
Unable to present
Because there is nothing to offer
Heart in pain
The Lord will know

Not being able to give because unable to offer
Empty
Hollow heart
Lonely, in agony, hurting
Absent-mindedly forming tears
Till wishing to at least offer the heart
That wants to give on a silver plate gently placed
Looking up to the blue autumn skies
With pure and innocent tear drops glistening
Deer-like saints
The Lord will help

For the coming Thanksgiving Day
An earnest plea
To please the beloved Shepherd
Spirits filled with ardent desire
The Lord will guide

Though having nothing to offer
Not a miserly heart ungiving
But willing to give
Though not having anything to offer
Only over such heart of pure love
The Lord will rejoice
Will receive with pleasure

On the Thanksgiving Day
Is the heart that is acceptable

Manwoo A. Kim

"A Thankful Heart"
(November 11, 2002)

A thankful heart
A God-given heart
A beautiful heart

In it is perched the noble image of Jesus
Clear and lucid, pure
Like crystal sea of glass
That great God's grace reflecting
How the love of the cross becomes visible

Autumn's field road
Ripened five grains
And flowers of the field
Fall leaves
Resplendent with five cardinal colors
Shining by the sunrays
Combed with the setting sun
Are blessings He gives
In the back road of life

Wanting to praise, wishing to sing
Desiring to extol, willing to sing chorus
Heart that cannot contain itself
Overflowing with richness
The beloved Shepherd fills to the brim
The skies appear even more high and blue
How merry, trodding on the spiritual lane

Ye who love Jesus
Come out to the First Pasture opening the Harvest Banquet
The past year's fruits in twelve baskets fill up
Won't you offer to the altar of the holy Lord?

The God-given heart of love
Heart that knows thankfulness
Feeling a lack no matter how much offered
And offered again
Going around and around the altar area
Walking up and down restlessly

New Morning of the Pasture

Until falling on the knees prostrate
The godly saint
Over whose shoulders descending the autumnal leaves
How they are like the hand touch of God the Father

Fruits of the Gospel and the harvest offertory
Presented together with Thanksgiving praise
With heart kicking with joy offering to the Lord
The morning of the Thanksgiving Day
Is so very joyful and good

Manwoo A. Kim

"A New Morning Has Brightened"
(November 24, 2002)

A new morning has brightened
A morning overflowing with thanksgiving has come
The past one year has been for this day

God who created us in His own image
Jesus who made us a new creation
Holy Spirit who leads us
In the life of heavenly citizens

That He forgives our sins and transgressions
Hears our prayers
Gives us five grains and flowers of the fields
Makes the Gospel preached to all the world
Till now enables us to serve the Lord
And live by faith
Let us thank

Open our hearts, part our lips, expand our bosoms
The great love of the exalted God
His everlasting blessing, grace, long-suffering
Let us thank

That He has guided, guarded, and protected us to here
When falling down and fainting has lifted us up
When making mistakes, failing and stumbling
Has forgiven
When wandering from left to right has held us fast
When trapped in a dilemma has brought us out
On the Rock of Ages has firmly established us
Let us thank

Let us all together sing hymns of thanksgiving
Let us sing joyful songs to the living, powerful Father
Upon the saints
Gathering on the Thanksgiving Lord's Day morning
Worshiping
May great blessing abundant be
Days
Overflowing spiritually and physically
Are approaching
Let us thank

New Morning of the Pasture

"If Wind Does Not Blow"
(December 1, 2002)

If wind does not blow
Fallen leaves will not dance

Blown by the wind
Like leaves over the asphalt
Smartly dancing and vanishing into somewhere
Having embraced hope
Budded on spring trees
Shown dark bluish-green tint all summer long
Like leaves yellowed by exposure to light
Souls wearied within time of comings and goings

If the wind of the Holy Spirit blows
Revived and renewed
Will dance

Like David joyously traversing through palace streets
For the living powerful Father God's glory to be revealed
Playing instruments and drums
Lifting voices
Will sing and dance robustly

Even in the First Pasture
Holy Spirit's wind, come ye blowing
Into souls listless like dried leaves
And crouching
From body chilled by late autumn's cold frost
So will they dance

Like autumnal leaves
Banded together
And doing the dance of the crowd
Let us all go out to the green pasture
Be blown by the wind of the Holy Spirit
To glorify our Lord
Let us dance the holy dance

Awaiting the day over there in eternal heaven
When we with angels will praise and dance
Standing at the corner of autumn's final exit
Like people intoxicated with the Holy Spirit
Let us to the tune of heaven, dance

Manwoo A. Kim

"The Day Of The General Assembly"
(December 8, 2002)

The day of the General Assembly
When baptized, confirmed members
With new members, catechists
And infant baptized saints gather
In the Lord look back over the past one year
And settle accounts

Despite having lived with all due diligence
Served faithfully
Wrestled to love the Lord with passion
A year with lack remaining

Toward the grace and love God has bestowed
The greater the thankfulness and emotion
Ashamed of life bespeckled with stinginess
Languor, excuses, doubt and grumbling
A year with pain remaining

Cannot but repent

The day of the General Assembly
When baptized, confirmed members
With new members, catechists
And infant baptized saints gather
In the Lord looking forward to the coming year
And plan budget

What kind of new blessings
Will He give in the new year?
When He blesses
Is the bowl to receive ready
The form of the beloved Shepherd
Striving to fill up
Like in the Garden of Gethsemene of blood-sweat
Pouring and praying
To the prepared heart
The year to be full of blessings

Cannot but believe

New Morning of the Pasture

Settling accounts with grief, lamentation
Confession and repentance
Planning the budget with hope, faith
Confidence and trust
From a fruit-bearing church to a harvesting church
Will He lead

To the right hand of the living and powerful Father God
I entrust the church
Bought with the precious blood

Manwoo A. Kim

"Because So Dirty And Filthy"
(December 15, 2002)

Because so dirty and filthy
So terrible to see and shabby it seemed
Could not just leave it
Observe no matter how
To leave it as it is He could not
So in the whole land all over the country
Here and there
Large flakes of snow
Like the beautiful disposition of the Creator God
Does He scatter

Even the haggard winter trees
Leaves having fallen
Seem as if wearing padded clothes
Over there where the fallen autumnal leaves
Pitiable from being trampled underfoot
With accumulation
Is pure
Like the whole world made into one
Clear, clean within
Calm stillness, gorgeous
It is as if the earnest desire in the hearts of souls
Tossed about in the storms of life
Filling up and flowing over
Once having completed
Far and long itinerary of chastity's narrow path
Is now finding its destination
In the world of the Other Side
How good it is

On the hill of Calvary the event that occurred
For the whole human race
Souls dirtied
To be made spotless
He who tore flesh and sprinkled blood
The beloved Shepherd
As if resembling His cherished desire
Falling winter's first snow

New Morning of the Pasture

For my faith, works, heart and life also
To be washed by the precious blood
Covered by the righteousness of the holy God
Like the wholly snow-covered mountains
Streams, plants and grass
Luminous, pure white become
And on this land polluted by the libertine culture
How I want to liberally disperse
The voluminous snowflakes of the Gospel

With God's divine favor like big flakes of snow
Over all the First Pasture descending
To make white wool of sheep flock even whiter
How I want to greet the new morning
Of the incandescent Garden

Just then
The rising sun of righteousness
Over it will brightly shine

How exquisite

Manwoo A. Kim

"As Christmas Fast Approaches"
(December 12, 2002)

One day as Christmas fast approaches
That Jesus who after the cross, resurrection
And ascension on the right hand of the heavenly throne
Offered intercessory prayers
Leaves the Land of Glory
As on the first Christmas night
Glory to God in the highest
And on earth peace to men on whom His favor rests
To call souls careworn from the libertine culture
Comes to the city
Brewing with drugs, violence, lewdness
Fraud, threat, menace, impurity and corruption
Is it because where sin abounds
Grace abounds even more
Is it because of the will of God the Father
Who rejoices more over one sinner repenting
Than 99 righteous

Past the ghastly back alleys dirtied by graffiti
Trash and garbage
Within a household
Seen through a battered window
Is not even one common Christmas item
A few tiny children poor-looking
Are squatting in front of an old, used TV set
Absorbed in card-playing
Venerable church buildings
Standing erect in the alleyways
Are as if they had weathered a storm
The cross once aloft the steep bell tower
Gone without a trace
Even the sounds of chime bells
That echoed the Christmas carols
Altogether ceased
To the taverns, offices
Warehouses and movie theatres
To temples of idols transformed
How desolate

New Morning of the Pasture

In every department store
Flickering with iridescent neon signs
The sound of auspicious footsteps
On the walls exhibiting all kinds of products
To lure customers in the Christmas climax
Or inside the picturesque cards neatly arranged
In the showcase in front of the wall
The words
Happy Holiday
Merry Christmas
Happy Hanuka
Happy Qwanza
The noisy tune of Jingle Bells
Ringing to entice shoppers
But Jesus is coming

Among the saints
Caught in the procession of numerous people
Departing the city without regret
Having found a residence
Quiet, safe, beautiful and nice to live in
Even if they met with Jesus of Christmas
Toward the city entering
Like Peter along the Road of Appia
Fleeing persecutions and suffering
Turning his back on Rome
Asking *Quo vadis*
Lord where are you going
There is none
Carrying pain starker
Than the loneliness experienced that time
That night in the nocturnal streets of Bethlehem
As when He riding on the donkey
To face suffering
Went up to Jerusalem and wept
Saying
Do not weep for me
Weep for yourselves and for your children
And went up the hill of Golgotha
To bear the cross
As the time of the Christmas holiday is approaching
Is He toward the city in silence walking in

O Lord, where are you going?

Manwoo A. Kim

"As King Of Kings"
(December 22, 2002)

As King of kings
Lord of lords
Savior of sinners
In the virgin Mary
Conceived by the Holy Spirit
Wearing the corpus of man
In Bethlehem stable's manger was born

Though into the world His handiwork
To the land of His own He had come
Yet was there no snug room to lay His frame

To make us rich
Form made poor
Whenever
The holiday commemorating the Holy Birth arrives
Because anew
Heart awe-stricken

Once again straightening oneself
And searching the grace received
Body saved from sin and death
Eternal life
Given in the grace of freedom from condemnation
Having become God's children
Promise of answers to prayer
Powerful work of fulfillment according to faith
Are all beyond description

Even on this year's Christmas fest
Will He let white snow flurry the First Pasture
With footsteps distinct
The beloved Shepherd will come
And as in the first Christmas receive praise

The hands of the junior and senior high students
Going out for Christmas caroling
Will He grasp and lead
Each and every saint coming to worship

New Morning of the Pasture

Will He embrace
The spirits
Concealing loneliness and lonesomeness
Inside their winter overcoats
Tightly sealing their lips to stifle sobbing
Swallowing tears and not knowing where to go
Will He soothe

Though in a shabby form He came
The babe Jesus, Immanuel God is He
The one and only begotten Son of God
The master of the First Pasture
If like Bethlehem, like the stable, like the manger
We can receive Him
A joyous Christmas Day it will be

Manwoo A. Kim

"As On First Christmas' Dawn"
(December 25, 2002)

On the day
Commemorating the birth of the Savior

As on first Christmas' dawn
The shepherds who hastened toward the manger

From far, far away land
Following a strange star
Over mountains and across the streams
With gold, frankincense and myrrh
Like the wise men of the East
Who hurried to where the baby Jesus was laid

During midnight
Like the angels who sang
Glory to God in the highest
And peace on earth to men on whom His favor rests

We, also arising
Toward the manger in the First Pasture on Mt. Tabor
Should praise
Present offering
Kneel down and adore Him

On the road returning
Good news of great joy that shall be for all the people
Should we proclaim
Today
In the town of David a Savior has been born to you
He is Christ the Lord
We shall shout

So that from Philadelphia
To all over the American continent
To the five oceans and the six continents
To the imprisoned inside tents of iron
Piercing through closely shut hearts
To many spirits, it would ring out

New Morning of the Pasture

Savior Jesus Christ
The one and only begotten Son of God
Wherever that beautiful name is heard
To God be the glory
The work of revival will begin

Joy to the world the Lord is come
Let earth receive her King!

Manwoo A. Kim

"Though Wanting To Go Back"
(December 29, 2002)

Though wanting to go back
Days passed
To a point of no return
When irretrievable one year
Changes to an old year

Though not wanting to go back
Time closing in that cannot but turn back
When one year of inevitable return
Transitions to a new year

Fearful emotions
Seeing the old year out and the new year in
Have a sense of lack and expectations
Reflection and prospecting are busy

Standing at the point
When the hour of running back to the past
And the time coming to the future
Touch each other
Gathering together to give the moments
Where the present appears subsumed in the past
And the future within the present
To the master of time, the sovereign Creator God
Administering the Communion
To put off the worn out clothes
And to wear new clothes
Upon the terminal station of history
Connecting to eternity I look

Though wanting to grasp
Out of reach
Though wanting to let go
Not escaping grasp
Though wanting to go back to the past
Distressed at the times flowing away
From last new year's morning
The beloved Shepherd who had been with us
I commit the coming new year

New Morning of the Pasture

Old things to new things start anew
The sun as always rises again
As to let the flock of sheep awaiting the morning
When the more the old things are forgotten
Are made anew
Try to live anew when nothing is new under the sun
The sheep
He with his nail pierced hand
Reaches out to grasp

Cherishing the hope of heart-beating
And looking at the new heaven and the new earth
Standing at the crevice
Where old to new are crossing
Appreciating
Where old things to new things
New things to old things converting
Passing the old year
I want to greet the new year

Old year, farewell
New year, hello

Manwoo A. Kim

"The Harvest Of The New Heaven and The New Earth"
(January 1, 2003)

The two faces of time
One to reflect upon the past
The other to look forward to the future

Though different in direction
Continuity keeping up onward to oneness

Yesterday, tomorrow's head runner
Tomorrow, yesterday's successor
In between today
Like an adhesive that combines the two
Which by forming a sense of time
The old year exits
And a new year comes again

The morning of the new year
Since it calls to mind the creation's new morning
And prompts a look toward the new heaven
And the new earth's morning
To the saints believing in Jesus Christ as Savior
And born anew
Living a new life
Is ever new

When in the eastern side of the sky
Aloft the bright sun rises
In the bosom welling up
Faith
Hope
Love
To harvest during the new year
A heart praying

To the beloved Shepherd
Always come looking to the First Pasture
The garden of blessing
A heart begging

New Morning of the Pasture

Bless
Send divine favor
On the new morning of new year's day
May it be a church that harvests
As if picking and placing the twelve fruits
Born all year around by the river of life
In the twelve baskets to overflowing
Because of soul's abundant harvest
Giving thanksgiving, praise and glory
To the living and powerful God
May the year 2003 be

Manwoo A. Kim

"Harvesting Church In This Land"
(January 1, 2003)

Meanwhile his disciples urged him, "Rabbi, eat something." But he said to them, "I have food to eat that you know nothing about." Then his disciples said to each other, "Could someone have brought him food?" "My food," said Jesus, "is to do the will of him who sent me and to finish his work. Do you not say, 'Four months more and then the harvest? I tell you, open your eyes and look at the fields! They are ripe for harvest. Even now the reaper draws his wages, even now he harvests the crop for eternal life, so that the sower and the reaper may be glad together. Thus the saying 'One sows and another reaps' is true. I sent you to reap what you have not worked for. Others have done the hard work, and you have reaped the benefits of their labor." (John 4:31-38)

We thank God for His grace of allowing us to see the old year go and the new year come in. We also thank God for His favor upon us in the past year and for the opportunity, health and faith to live for the Lord yet another year. The theme for our church this year is 'Harvesting Church in this Land.' The passage we read this morning contains an important message regarding harvest.

1) First, the passage tells us in verse 35 that **now** is a time of harvest. In I Corinthians 6:2, we read, "now is the time of God's favor, now is the day of salvation." Now refers to the time between Jesus' ascension and his second coming. We see the Bible referring to this period of time as the last days. While we live during the last days, it is also our present. The year 2003 is a now in the midst of our lives. May we make this new year a year of harvest.

2) Second, harvesting refers to **doing God's will and finishing his work** (vs. 34). We read in the Bible that it is not God's will that even one soul perishes. God wants all men to be saved and come to the knowledge of the truth (I Timothy 2:4). Those who say, "Lord, Lord," must act according to the Lord's will. May we make the new year a year of harvest to do God's will and His work.

3) Third, we read in verse 32 that the work of harvest is **required**, as is eating. Jesus considered harvesting necessary like the food He consumed. Jesus was so engrossed in the work of harvest that he did not even have a chance to eat with his disciples, as we see in Mark 6:31. To say that one does the work of harvest like eating is to emphasize the necessity of doing the work. We read in II Corinthians

11:27 that for the harvest of the spreading the Gospel, Apostle Paul often went without sleep, knew hunger and thirst, skipped meals, and was cold and naked. It is because of such bearers of the gospel that we too have been harvested as the people of heaven. May we harvest regularly as we eat in the new year.

4) Fourthly, we read in versus 36-38 that harvesting involves **reaping** what has been prepared for harvest. God chose in love those to be saved before the beginning of time. Jesus died on the cross and rose again in order for the chosen people to believe and be saved. The Holy Spirit works with those who proclaim the message of evangelism and stirs faith in the hearts of the chosen people who listen to God's Word. The people who live on this earth have been confronted with the Gospel, either directly or indirectly. What we do is harvesting the ripe grain that God has already prepared. The ripened grain awaits the time of harvest. May we in the new year be harvesters who harvest what has been prepared.

5) Finally, verse 36 of today's passage tells us that harvest is something over which both God and the harvesters **rejoice**. Jesus said that he greatly rejoices over one sinner repenting and returning to God. In Philippians 4:1 we see that the saints who have become God's children after repenting of sins and believing in Jesus Christ are referred to as the beloved, those longed for, joy and crown. Harvesting pleases God and makes our joy abundant. God said that He is delighted with the saving of souls through evangelism.

May the new year be filled with the joy of harvest.

May this year also be overflowing with physical harvest, along with spiritual harvest. May harvest be abundant in our life, faith, family, children, business, and work.

God has called us to be harvesters.

Manwoo A. Kim

"A New Morning Of Daybreak"
(January 5, 2003)

A new morning of daybreak
When another year of anticipation begins

Over the 100-year immigration history
Of the white-clad folk
Having taken the first step
In a small island of American territory
In the land of opportunity
Having left the native country
Beginning to dim with dark shadows
Of danger from foreign power
Considerations of terror, famine
Disease and hatred from war
I look back

In an alien land
Though could not speak
About all the suffered hardships
Coughing up prayers
For independence of the fatherland
Solicitude for enlightenment of free democracy
And sincere desire
For the reunification of the North and the South
As the light from the east, not a spot ashamed
Pouring blood sweat
Having lived through one many years
Anonymous fellow brethren's wearied footsteps
Though vanished
Here and there
Foot traces remaining like morning star are shining

Fellow countrymen let us now arise
Standing in the world's stage of the twenty-first century
Into the darkening conscience of humanity
Let us light the torch of justice
Truth, freedom and peace
The Korean Diaspora

* Beginning of the 100th Anniversary year of Korean Immigration to the United States of America

New Morning of the Pasture

Hand in hand
Making a sash to tightly bind and pull up the earth
Let all over the world receive sunbeams indiscriminately
With the holy will of heaven remaining
Body and soul rich
Contributing to the history of mankind
A people of heaven it will be

The new morning of the 100th anniversary
Of Korean immigration to the U.S.
For the fellow brethren taking root in this land
A year of great divine favor it is

Manwoo A. Kim

"Last Night"
(January 12, 2003)

Last night
As the winter tree in the First Pasture
By violent northern gale
Stood shivering, its bosom cold
Sending down white divine favor
He with a cotton garment it clothed

Washed by the precious blood
Like pure, white new ceremonial attire
New year's morning

Preparation to meet the One coming to seek
The beloved Shepherd
Leaving white footprints

Dazzling

I will worship prostrate
Raising voice, praise
Dance

The closer before His presence
Him more resembling
Clean, clear heart
The winter tree appearing more immaculate
On every haggard branch
Fully blooming snow-flowers
Having received morning sunbeams
Brilliantly gleaming
In the Lord's garden
Big blessings will be

Glory of Zion
Evermore
Will shine

The winter pasture is
Very
White
Stainless

"The Winter Sea"
(January 19, 2003)

The winter sea
When with cold wind whirling
Waves in consternation
Over sidewalk nearly devoid of any human trace
Lonely waterfowls whose feeble crying
Is only heard

Shepherd of love
Where are you?
When are you coming?
What are you doing?
When shouting and writhing?
One small soul
Looking up to the lead-colored heaven
Seeming to freeze over
Cries out

When from the chimney of a small fishing boat
Smoke emitted in rings
Forcefully plowing its way
Through wild raging waves
Appears hollow

From there beyond the remote horizon
Suddenly shooting up
New year's morning sun light
Over the whole sea shining
Drawing a beautiful landscape
Is because
Even if suffering from all kinds of illnesses
In sadness, pain and heartbreak beyond control
Souls trembling
Jesus the sun of righteousness
Our utmost beloved Shepherd
Is in the midst of life
Enables the drawing of a brilliant life's picture
To make us realize

Manwoo A. Kim

Like the morning sun of the winter sea
Beloved Shepherd, come
Let the golden light resplendent five grains
And flowers of the field
Ripen in the First Pasture
That this year
One of harvesting in this land may be

New Morning of the Pasture

"Winter Night"
(January 26, 2003)

Winter night
High aloft in the sky
Over the shoulders of the saints going home
With hearts full of grace
After the Wednesday prayer meeting
Remaining as bluish light
Making shadows
Moon

Even during midnight
When all the world seems to have frozen over
To the pilgrims longing for eternity
As an affection adoring God's Kingdom
Cozy air permeates

Like a shadow lengthening and shortening
Always abiding
Jesus the beloved Shepherd
Even during an easily icy season
In every bosom
Kindles the Holy Spirit's fire
And warms the souls
Pours in sincere prayer requests
Blazing like a smelting furnace
So that with prayer-heat boiling up
By the cries of the pure, innocent flock of sheep
Much regurgitated as hotness unmanageable
The First Pasture will certainly not freeze over

Only if the fire of the Gospel were kindled
In the bosoms of the pedestrians
Wearing clothes in layers and huddled over
Because of winter sky's cold wave
Then even in the gloomy back alley of Philadelphia
Warmth will circulate
Frozen Skuylkill river abate
Brimfully carrying a beautiful melody will flow

Manwoo A. Kim

The deeper the night becomes
When the shadows shorten with the waning of the moon
Floating high above in the midair
The more the believers pressing their footsteps
Look forward to that day
The more will their hearts be satisfied

Even in the cold winter night
By such great grace
Affectionate
Serene

"Winter Tree"
(February 2, 2003)

Winter tree
Though by violent gusts
Gaunt branches seem about to be broken off
Unfractured

Cold wind that chafes the skin
Rushing in
Even in a season when all is frigid
Unfrozen

Within ground gelid
Though
Roots difficult to absorb moisture are athirst
Un-dried

Because within perches the Creative life
Throughout the tree
Veins flow

Winter pilgrim
Though exhausted by the storms of life
Diseased, lonely
Writhing in frustration and discouragement
Finally fall like autumnal leaves
And seem to transform into a handful of dust
Body having received everlasting life
Has the covenant of resuscitation

When the footsteps of the beloved Shepherd are heard
With loving voice He beckons
For the winter trees of the First Pasture
Smitten by the frost
And trembling from the cold
As if accosting spring
A day of careless bursts of bluish smiles
And explosive laughs will be

There is no fear
Hope abounds

Manwoo A. Kim

No matter that bitter winter shiver crashes in
With the beloved Shepherd
Spring comes that much more
What is there to worry about

Even on the winter tree
Will there be a day of spring weather's descent

"Though Large Flakes Of Snow Covered"
(February 9, 2003)

Last night
Though large flakes of snow covered
Over the frozen ground
Earth
Underneath humbly breathing
Probably awaits a bright spring day

Spring rain, come as you may
Balmy wind, blow as you may
Snow will but melt
Gelid ground thaw
Just as hibernating animals are stretching themselves
And awakening
When the plow-holding farmers following pasture
Come and cultivate the field
Will there be a day?
When the buried earth sees the sunbeams

When with hoe, shovel
Harrow, and weeding hoe
Caressing the gentle hands
Touch
Soil will become soft, cushiony
Preparing for budding
And much better would it be
If over that at least a drizzle is sprinkled

At last
Will appear they who scatter seeds
Those who prune
Water, fertilize
And weed will show up
When flowered, born of fruits, and ripened deliciously
The Harvester must come

Even in the First Pasture
The sounds of spring
From over there
Are beginning to be heard

Manwoo A. Kim

But where are the Kingdom workers?
When will the stewards faithful until death arrive?
Who will come and whom will He send?
Though not perfect
Those after the heart of the beloved Shepherd
He will fill with the Spirit
Faith, grace, wisdom, power
Commendation and angelic face
Choose and establish

I really believe
I pray

New Morning of the Pasture

"Selecting Ordained Deacons"
(February 16, 2003)

We thank God for His grace.
Next Lord's Day we will be holding a General Assembly to select seven prospective ordained deacons. The whole congregation participates in the General Assembly, but only the confirmed members vote for the deacons. Those 65 years old or under in both the English and Korean congregations who have served as acting deacons for at least three years are candidates, and among them seven are chosen. Among those who can vote, each would circle the name(s) of the desired seven or fewer deacons listed on the ballot card. Those with at least two-thirds of the vote will be chosen.

I hope that we will all be praying during this week and asking God to put into our hearts the names of the seven deacons. The qualifications for an ordained deacon are found in I Timothy 3 and Acts 6. Korean Christianity's faith tradition emphasizes abstention from alcohol, smoking, drugs, gambling and double life as well as keeping the Lord's Day, worship, tithing, and a life of prayer, evangelism, and Bible-centeredness. By voting for ordained deacons we are choosing Kingdom workers for our church. Despite inadequacies of the candidates, we choose those whom we believe God will nurture and use.

The selected to-be-ordained deacons are trained once every week for six months and are ordained after passing the examination by the Session of Elders. The Holy Spirit's special grace is present during the ordination. More so than the acting deacon, the ordained deacon washes the feet of the flock and serves the church with double duty and fervor. Of sincere desires of a saved male saint should be the desire to be ordained as a deacon. The ordained deacons serve for life.

During the General Assembly this coming Sunday, may there be grace of accomplishing God's holy work by the candidates and voters together, and may we harvest seven prospective ordained deacons.

Manwoo A. Kim

"Today Is A Happy Day"
(February 23, 2003)

Today is a happy day
A day of joyful rest

A blessed day when God receiving adoration
And saints worshiping
Meet within the Word

Though by snowstorm once so intimidating
Snow-mountain piled high
Stands to obstruct the way to church
It is as if it melts
Unable to endure the sunbeams
Warming in late winter
Likewise
After the Lord's Day morning worship
When praising, praying
And giving offering are enjoyed to the fullest
Hearts cleansed
With sin's knots one by one washed by the precious blood

Facing the voting on the day of the General Assembly
Those seeking God's will
In order to choose stewards of the vineyard
According to prayer preparations

Who God's chosen workers are
Who are after God's heart
Who will say, "Here am I, send me"
Though we do not know
The Shepherd knows

Grant us a deacon like Stephen
A deacon like Philip
In Your Providence make known
May they be chosen
Train them and use them
May fruit-bearing be
Receive glory
We plead

New Morning of the Pasture

For this church in this land
To be a harvesting church
Give us heavenly workers
In the First Pasture
Regretful for a dearth of workers
When harvest is plenty
Send seven deacons to be ordained
Make them workers
With spring briskly approaching
Make faithful harvesters
Who will handle the sheep pen
Tend to the fruit tree
Cultivate the land

That You will give
We believe
To the outcome
We submit
Only
May Your will be done

Manwoo A. Kim

"Spring, Spring, Spring"
(March 2, 2003)

Spring, spring, spring
Spring it is
Even in the First Pasture spring has come
It has come indeed

Cloudy weather having cleared
Cozy spring beams remain
Frozen ground turns warm
Even range after range
Snow heaps like mountain high melt down
Already
Cattails put forth fuzzy bud fringes
In forsythia's eyes yellow light breaks out
Even field feline with vivacity dart off
Spring energy is evident

All winter long
Trapped inside the pen
Within dark, depressing time
Huddled trembling
White, incandescent sheep awaiting a bright spring!
Run out to the greening pasture
Let us go and receive the beloved Shepherd
Hastening from there over the hill

Pulled along by our Shepherd
Singing joyous hymns
Scattering seeds of flowers
That will regurgitate fragrance
Where love, forgiveness
Patience and peace
In each for others embracing
Are perched
Let us yet again tend to our pasture

Finally
For life to come out
From light drizzle's permeating ground
Pain of skin bursting out

New Morning of the Pasture

Sorrow of inside flesh rotting
Labor pains of head pushing out
And roots going down the soil
Sound of water streaming up
Within the small branches
Blood-flow
Rhythmic movements' colorfully brilliant symphony
Will be performed

Now
Our First Pasture
Together with the Shepherd of love
Greets a glorious spring

How happy
How very good

Rev. Manwoo A. Kim started writing poetry since his college days at Yonsei University in Seoul, Korea. Since then Rev. Kim has written thousands of poems.

Rev. Manwoo A. Kim with his father, Rev. Hee Do Kim, who served many years as the Senior Pastor of Bu-Pyeong Church in Busan, South Korea. Rev. Hee Do Kim preached actively after retirement right up to his death.

Rev. Manwoo A. Kim married the first (and the only) love of his life, Sooeun, who is the first daughter of the famous preacher, Rev. In Sun Jun, who was martyred for his Christian faith during the Korean War. Tong-Hap Presbyterian Church (a major Presbyterian denomination in Korea) is currently in the process of compiling a record of his martyrdom for their Korean Martyrs Pilgrimage project.

Rev. Manwoo A. Kim was ordained as a Minister of the Christian Gospel by the Ko-Shin Presbyterian Church (a big Presbyterian denomination in South Korea).

This family photo was taken during the early years of Rev. Manwoo A. Kim's pastoral ministry in Suh Moon Church in Seoul, Korea. Rev. Kim was the Senior Pastor of Suh Moon Church until he immigrated to the USA in 1979.

Manwoo A. Kim

The Korean Diaspora's Realized Vision
(Focus on the Work of Missions in North America)
Rev. Manwoo Kim

In the spring of 1979 when my ministry was in South Korea, I was invited to speak for a revival at the First Korean Presbyterian Church in Philadelphia. After speaking at the revival, I had the opportunity to observe the Korean immigration society and Korean churches in America. Korean immigration then being in its prime, Korean communities and churches were here and there being formed and established. At that time about 20,000-30,000 Koreans were entering the United States every year. In Philadelphia, Pennsylvania, about 10,000 Koreans and 20 immigration churches were already established. The city of Philadelphia was the first city that received and protected the freed slaves after President Abraham Lincoln had declared emancipation but the Southern white landowners were recapturing them. Even today in various parts of the city one can take a tour of many places that are vestiges retracing the historical footprints of the black people. In an area in Philadelphia's vicinity resides a black middle class of considerable social standing, formed by former slaves who came to Philadelphia following the emancipation and were advancing in society as free citizens. At that time as I visited Philadelphia, New York, Washington D.C., and Toronto, Canada, I received several strong challenges:

1) Because the concentration of the Korean immigrants coming in droves centered on the Korean church, there was a great need for the establishment of proper viewpoint of the church, pastoring, theology, and missions of the Korean churches

2) For the cooperation of different Korean churches, there was a need for a cooperative body

3) For the future of the Korean community and the second and third generation Korean-Americans, there was a need from the initial stages of Korean immigration for a Christian students movement (like SFC) geared towards youth activities, in order to nurture leadership figures for tomorrow's church and world

4) Because life's arena for Koreans in the beginning of immigration was generally in the Harlem area (in New York) or areas with heavy concentration of black people, a normalization of Korean/African-American relationship was the most urgent duty

5) Because of American wealth and leadership role in international politics and its position of sending the most missionaries to the world, the outpost of world missions can only be in America

As soon as I realized these facts, they continued in my mind and gave rise to further ideas. I ruminated upon them, until they resulted in some kind of a resolution. After finishing the American revival in May of 1979 and returning to Korea, my mind was already made up. As soon as I arrived in Korea, I discussed with my family regarding moving my ministry from Korea to America, and my wife was in positive agreement. Therefore we prayed, and during that time we opportunely received an invitation from this church that I am now serving. Thinking it as God's will, I was sent as a missionary to North America from the General Assembly of the Korean Presbyterian Church in Korea (Koshin) to which I belong, and that same year on the thirteenth of November my family immigrated to the U.S. I was then inaugurated as the Senior Pastor of First Korean Presbyterian Church of Philadelphia (FKPCP). After inauguration, by God's grace, we were able to purchase a church building in a location comprised of 50% white and 50% black population, and afterwards on June 30, 1986 we purchased the current building. For seven years we renovated it as a church building, dedicated it, have been advancing the Lord's work full-scale, and began to unfold the vision I had when I was coming to America.

The work that has been progressing during this time can be summarized as follows:

1) We have developed the Student For Christ (SFC) movement since 1979 in order to nurture leaders in the Korean-American society and church and for the spiritual training of the second and third generation Korean-Americans. At first, Rev. Jae Young Park led the first conference in the U.S. east coast in August of 1979. About 40 churches and 500 students attended. In November of the same year, I was entrusted with the position as the General Secretary and subsequently served. Then in 1984 the Korean Presbyterian Church (Koshin) in America was organized, and it entrusted me with the position as the Chairman of the Supervisory Committee, and I have continually served to develop this movement. Currently SFC is active in North and South American Continents; in the six areas in North America (American east coast, west coast, northwest, mid-south, and south, and Canada). Junior and senior high conferences are held every summer and college and junior/senior high conferences every winter. For 23 years about 20,000 students were touched by the SFC movement. The SFC movement has produced missionaries, pastors, theologians, and lay leaders who have been making their way into the American mainstream society.

The SFC movement holds evangelical, conservative theology, Reformed faith, spirit of martyrdom, and repentance movement as the spirit of its faith, and holds faithfulness to scholarship, Bible study, prayer life, personal witnessing, campus evangelism, and the establishment of the Reformed faith churches as its realizing goals which have been continued. From 1998, every four years we hold a national conference. In the first conference about 1000 youths of a national proportion gathered in Los Angeles, California; four years later in 2002, July 30-August 2, about 1500 students from South America, Canada, Korea, China, and the whole breadth of North America gathered at the campus of the University of Villanova, in the suburbs of the city of Philadelphia. The theme of this second national conference was "Arise and Shine". During this time youths received great challenges and much blessing.

Spurred by the SFC movement three other big movements have arisen in the Korean-American community.

2) We participated and dedicated ourselves as a promoter and charter member for three organizations formed to provide a wholesome direction and concentration of the Korean-American churches.

   (a) The formation of the Council of Korean Churches of the Greater Philadelphia began during the SFC conference in August 15, 1980 in the Rosemont College campus. Rev. John Kim, Rev. Henry Koh, Rev. Han Ku Yuh and I sat together and discussed the need for such a body. We resolved to summon a promotion committee. We thereafter dispatched an official document to all the churches in the Greater Philadelphia area in September of 1980. Of the 20 churches then founded, 16 churches responded and participated, and the Council was formed. The first president was Rev. Ki Hang O, who was pastoring the first Korean Church in Philadelphia. In the fall of the same year, the first Evangelistic Revival was held in a Methodist church in South Philadelphia.

   There are presently (in 2003) 200 Korean churches in this area, of which 100 are participating member churches. Every year in the fall are held evangelistic revivals for both the first generation Koreans and the second generation (English speaking). The Council also holds the New Year's Prayer Breakfast (inviting Korean, African-American, Caucasian, and Latin-American political and religious leaders), Easter

Day Combined Early Rise Worship (in the public square in front of Philadelphia city's Art Museum), and worship services in commemoration of March 1 and Korean Independence. With the organizations in Korean community we are making a concerted effort for the Korean-American community to penetrate into the American mainstream society. Through the Church Council, there is an active interchange between the Korean society and the American society, which is of great benefit to the Korean-American community.

(b) Founding of the Korean Presbyterian Church in America. Just as important as a united movement is a church-movement that is Bible-centered and has Reformed faith. For such a movement we propelled the founding of the denomination with fellow workers in America. Rev. Hong Kwon Jung, myself, Rev. Jae Young Park, and Rev. Keun Sam Lee initiated it and afterwards Rev. Hyun Kuk Shin joined forces. We advanced from 1982, adopted the Westminster Confession of Faith, formed a synod in November of 1984 with a group of churches grounded in the Reformed faith, and afterwards promoted into the General Assembly (with six presbyteries). Presently we have advanced to 100 churches and 150 pastors. Since then until now, we have developed into a God-centered, Bible-centered, church-centered, correct theology and pastoring movement.

(c) In 1988 in Los Angeles there was a meeting binding all the Korean churches in American regions. I attended this meeting and our church participated as the organizing committee and founding member of the Korean World Mission of Christ (KWMC), and I currently serve as a co-chair. This KWMC has held a missions conference in Chicago's Billy Graham Center every four years since 1988, where 4000 Koreans gather. These include 800 Korean missionaries who have been sent as missionaries for at least four years, as well as attendants ranging from Sunday school children to adults. It is a missions conference like the Passover of Korean missions: Korean missions leaders scattered throughout Korea, America and the rest of the world as well as world-oriented missions scholars and those in charge of the missions department in each church attend. Through the KWMC for the past 15 years many second generation Korean-American missionaries were produced, and they have greatly contributed to the world missions of Korean churches and to Korean missionaries' globalization. It is probably not an overstatement to say that presently the KWMC is managing a central role for 4000 Korean churches' missions movement abroad.

This year from February 4-6 in Hawai, the missions conference in Hawai marked the 100th anniversary of Korean immigration to America. About 2000 participants gathered under the collaborative auspices of KWMC, Korea World Missions Association (KWMA) and Hawai's church association. Korea's KWMA had been organized under the influence of America's KWMC. One person who played an instrumental role in both was Rev. Il Shik Choi. The present KWMC General Secretary, Rev. Suk Hee Koh, and KWMA's General Secretary, Rev. Seung Sam Kang, are committed and exerting their efforts.

3) Korean- and African-American relationship and combined worship

   (a) The beginning of combined Korean- and African-American services started with an invitation to the church music festival once we had procured a church building in May of 1980 in an area where residents were divided roughly equally between the white and black populations. This was the first such combined service in the Philadelphia area.

   (b) This combined service developed into street evangelism in the inner-city, where many African-American people live.

   (c) There was a further development into concentrated evangelism to four chosen areas of great African-American population every third Sunday from 1985.

   (d) Among the African-American churches we chose two churches for communion. With Holy Tabernacle Church we had combined street evangelism two times a year, and with Camphor Memorial United Methodist Church we have had combined worship once every year. We take turns holding the event in our church buildings, as an exchange visitation every other year. We had combined worship services, praise and worship programs, banquet feasts, cooking classes in Korean and American dishes, scholarship grants, and other programs. This year we have the 15th Korean- and African-

American combined worship; this year we visit the African-American church. At our 10th anniversary event, President Clinton and Pennsylvania's Governor Tom Ridge sent congratulatory remarks, and in 2002 we received a citation from the Council of the city of Philadelphia.

(e) Furthermore, we expanded our cooperative program agreement to have African-American church leaders visit Korea, as well as for African-American and Korean youths to visit Korea together - to build a greater friendship in Christ and to encourage mutual understanding. In 2000 I was in charge of the two-week trip to Korea with 20 African-American pastors, judge, and policemen as well as 10 Korean pastors, sponsored by the Myung Sung Church (Rev. Kim Sam-Whan). At that time we visited Korean churches, viewed church relics and observed the Korean industry. We also visited the Ool-san dockyard and toured the Hyundai automobile factory as well as the site where 10 ships were being constructed. Each of these ships weighs over 300,000 tons and is 10 stories high. They can each carry the whole population of Seoul. After these observations, the visitors admitted the following on our way back:

(i) They realized that Koreans came to America not because they could not make a living but for a better opportunity and to contribute to America

(ii) They were impressed by the passionate faith of the Korean churches and resolved to remember Korean Christian piety in their ministry and Christian work

(iii) Upon going up to the Korean church sanctuary area where the sermon is delivered and seeing that the preacher (and other church leaders) who entered that area took off their shoes, fellow visitors realized the significance of God's words "take off your shoes" to Moses and to Joshua, and one African-American church leader decided to do likewise in his church in the USA

(iv) The African-American leaders wanted more Korean- and African-American combined events, and they asked Korean churches to infuse vitality into American churches

Prior to this time, in May 26 of 1991, we were able to have a combined fellowship worship of the Council of Korean Churches of the Greater Philadelphia and the African-American Pastors' Association. Under the supervision of our church (FKPCP) we worshiped in an African-American church, the Zion Baptist Church, which has had a great political influence in the Philadelphia area. At that time I was asked to deliver the main address and I made the following thanksgiving and proposals:

(a) Thankfulness

   (i) Thankfulness to the black slaves, who had a leading part in the construction of America

   (ii) Thankfulness to the American blacks' civil rights movement, for bringing all kinds of benefits to the ethnic minorities. Thus, the more recent immigrants, the Koreans, have benefited

   (iii) Thankfulness for being the customers of Korean-owned stores, many of which are in black neighborhoods, for valuing them, and for greatly utilizing them

   (iv) Thankfulness to the many black soldiers who came during the Korean war, sacrificed themselves, and fought for free democracy so that a free Republic of Korea was possible and Korean churches were able to expand greatly

   (v) Thankfulness even now for greeting us warmly (white pastors and Korean pastors met for combined programs only twice in the past 22 years and were not able to continue)

(b) Proposals

   (i) For a regular meeting of Korean- and African-American leaders

   (ii) For a more systematic (and city-wide) organization of Korean- and African-American pastors and Korean- and African-American combined events

   (iii) For a more extensive Korea visitation program for Korean-and African-American leaders in Pennysylvania

(iv) For Korean- and African-American youths' exchange programs and joint Korea visitation (for the future leaders of the Korean- and African-American communities)

(v) For Korean- and African- American cultural exchange (for instance, Korean- and African-American pastors could take a one-day city tour of the historical footprints of the black people in America)

Our Council of Korean churches and the African-American Pastors' Association have adopted these proposals. Already Korean- and African-American youths have visited Korea together a few times, and Korean- and African-American leaders have continually visited Korea every year. Under God's grace, we are now already approaching our 15th combined Korean- and African-American worship service and 10th Korean- and African-American leaders' Korea visitation.

If at the time of the L.A. riots there were such a relationship and efforts toward friendship between the Korean- and African-American church leaders in the Greater Los Angeles area, it is possible that the riots could have been prevented. We actually see the role of the combined Korean- and African-American worship here as having prevented such a phenomenon in the Philadelphia area.

Not only with African-Americans, but also with Latin-American churches and other Asian and Caucasian churches, there is a demand for multi-racial combined events. Among our second-generation pastors there are many cases of those who already minister to different ethnic groups or are expanding to do so. Even in our church's English ministry, an African-American doctor, a Chinese/ Cambodian engineer's family, a Spanish family, Jewish-Christians, and Caucasians attend. This is one of the important programs which the future Korean church needs to think about in order to live and survive in this land.

4) World Missions

(a) Focusing on inner-city missions, we divided church districts into 20 missions districts in 1980. And each missions district was made to correspond to different parts of the world divided into 20. Each district is in charge of the respective areas for missions work.

(i) Presently we have commissioned three families of missionaries

（ii）　We have established and are managing a Gospel medical clinic in West Africa's Sierra Leon

(b) In 1982 we established a Korean church in the Middle East United Arab Emirates' Dubai, and I was inaugurated as the initial Senior Pastor. Recently the fifth pastor was appointed and the church was the first to have its own church building in the area.

    (i)　This Dubai church being the starting point, we support the Middle East Missionaries' Association (then five missionaries) currently with 400 Korean missionaries. I serve as a Supervisor of the association.

    (ii)　In the Philadelphia area, we organized the Middle East Missions Association (MEMA) whose representatives are encouraged to participate in the Middle East Missionaries' Missions Conference every two years.

    (iii)　In the Asian Center of Theological Seminary (ACTS) and College in Korea, a Middle East Missions Graduate School (MEMGS) was established, and missionary Chung Hyung-Nam (a long-time missionary in Jordan) is in charge and nurturing missionaries to the Middle East. I serve as a director for MEMGS.

(c) Rev. Doho Bang (missionary to Peru) and I promoted the Peru Koshin Missions Association, which started the Pastors' short-term theology training in 1999. This year we approach the fourth annual training. We are doing a cooperative work with the WEC ARM.

Looking back over the past 24 years, we see that God has given us the vision and dreams, the strength to realize it, the opportunity, good fellow workers, and the ability to work and to continue in accomplishing our dreams for His glory. This is entirely God's grace. We thank the Triune God for enabling us to work with tireless efforts until now. We thank the many prayer supporters, financial supporters, and partners. Particularly to the congregation of the First Korean Presbyterian Church of Philadelphia, I would like to express thankfulness, with a grateful heart.

Soli Deo Gloria!

February 20, 2003

www.ingramcontent.com/pod-product-compliance
Lightning Source LLC
LaVergne TN
LVHW011209080426
835508LV00007B/695